Speed Skating

BY LAURA HAMILTON WAXMAN

W9-BPR-427

AMICUS HIGH INTEREST • AMICUS INK

Amicus High Interest and Amicus Ink are imprints of Amicus
P.O. Box 1329, Mankato, MN 56002
www.amicuspublishing.us

Library of Congress Cataloging-in-Publication Data
Names: Waxman, Laura Hamilton, author.
Title: Speed Skating / by Laura Hamilton Waxman.
Description: Mankato Minnesota : Amicus Illustrated/Amicus
 Ink, 2018. | Series: Winter Olympic Sports | Includes
 bibliographical references and index. | Audience: Grade 4 to 6.
Identifiers: LCCN 2016042397 (print) | LCCN 2016054166
 (ebook) | ISBN 9781681511535 (library binding) | ISBN
 9781681521848 (pbk.) | ISBN 9781681512433 (ebook)
Subjects: LCSH: Speed skating–Juvenile literature. | Winter
 Olympics–Juvenile literature.
Classification: LCC GV850.3 .W39 2018 (print) | LCC
 GV850.3 (ebook) | DDC 796.91/4–dc23
LC record available at https://lccn.loc.gov/2016042397

Editor: Wendy Dieker
Series Designer: Kathleen Petelinsek
Book Designer: Aubrey Harper
Photo Researcher: Holly Young

Photo Credits:
ZUMA Press, Inc./Alamy Stock Photo cover; PCN
Photography/Alamy Stock Photo 4; Mary Evans/Sueddeutsche
Zeitung Photo 7; Rick Rickman/NewSport/ZUMAPRESS.
com/Alamy 8–9; PCN Photography/Alamy Stock Photo 11;
AP Photo/Kevin Frayer 12; AP Photo/Chris Carlson 15; PCN
Photography/Alamy Stock Photo 16; Jasper Juinen/Getty
Images 19; EMPICS Sport/PA Images/Alamy Stock Photo 20–
21; Harry E. Walker/MCT/Alamy Live News 23; Jeff Cable/
ZUMA Press, Inc./Alamy Stock Photo 24; Jasper Juinen/Getty
Images 26–27; epa european pressphoto agency b.v./Alamy
Stock Photo 28

Printed in the United States of America

HC 10 9 8 7 6 5 4 3 2 1
PB 10 9 8 7 6 5 4 3 2 1

Table of Contents

Going for the Gold   5

Long Track Skating   10

Short Track Skating   21

Go, Speed Racers!   29

Glossary   30

Read More   31

Websites   31

Index   32

South Korea's Bo Ra Lee takes off from the starting line in the 2014 Olympics.

Going for the Gold

The skaters get into starting position. Their bodies are tense and ready for action. Bang! They're off! The crowd roars as they fly around the track.

The world's fastest skaters face off every four years at the winter Olympics. They bring power, skill, and determination to the sport of speed skating.

Speed skating was part of the first winter Olympics in 1924. For years, all races took place on one kind of track. Today it's called the **long track**. It's a 400-meter (1,312-foot) loop. In 1992, **short track** races were added. The short track is the size of a hockey rink. One lap is about 111.1 meters (364.5 feet) long.

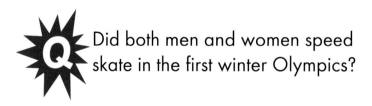
Q Did both men and women speed skate in the first winter Olympics?

In the 1936 Olympics, speed skating races were held outdoors on a frozen lake.

 Women racers were not allowed in those early years. But they won the right to compete in the 1960 Olympics.

Long track and short track skating take strength and balance. Body position is just as important. Skaters bend their knees to take longer and stronger strides. They also stay in the tuck position. This helps them have less **air resistance**. So does wearing a tight bodysuit. The bodysuit is made of a smooth, thin fabric. It helps the skater slice through the air.

US gold medalist Apolo Ohno stays tucked as he leads the pack.

Long Track Skating

Push, push, turn! In long track skating, two skaters race at a time. But they're not racing against each other. They're racing against the clock. Each skater's time is recorded. Skaters with the fastest times move on to the next round. The final round decides who wins the gold medal.

Two men race the clock as they skate
fast laps around the long track.

Long track speed skaters wear special skates and tight uniforms.

Q Are long track skates different from other kinds of skates?

In each race, one racer starts in the inner lane. This lane is the shortest. The other racer starts on the outer lane. It's a little longer. To keep things fair, the racers switch lanes during each lap. That way, they both end up skating the same total distance.

Yes! The boot of each skate is attached to the blade at the front. But the heel of the boot lifts away from the blade. This allows skaters to go faster.

Men and women each have five events for individual skaters. The shortest race is the 500 meter. That's a little more than once around the track. Another short race is the 1,000 meter. For these races, skaters must **sprint** with a huge burst of speed. Every movement counts. The top skater might win by just a hundredth of a second.

Shani Davis of the US chases South Korea's Mun Joon in the 1,000 meter race.

Marrit Leenstra from the Netherlands won a long track gold medal in the 2014 Olympics.

Q What is the country to beat in long track skating?

For men, the longest race is the 10,000 meter race. That's 25 laps around the track. For women, it's the 5,000 meter. That's 12.5 laps. These races take a mix of pacing and speed. Racers who go too fast risk tiring out and falling behind. But racers who start out too slow might never catch up. Skaters have to time things just right to finish with a good time.

 The Netherlands has won more long track skating Olympic medals than any other country. That's probably because they invented modern skating.

The team pursuit is on the long track. Two teams of three people race at a time. The teams start at opposite sides of the track. Bang! They take off. They try to catch the other team for six or eight laps. If one team passes the other, the race is over. Otherwise, the team with the best time goes to the next round.

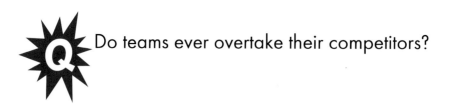 Do teams ever overtake their competitors?

The Canadian men's team sprints around the long track together in the team pursuit.

 Not very often. In 2006, a Japanese skater fell in the women's bronze-medal race. The Russians passed her and won the race.

Short Track Skating

A group of skaters zoom around a short track. One of them sprints ahead to take the lead! Short track skating pits four to five skaters against one another. There are no lanes. Skaters can switch positions throughout the race. The top two skaters of each race go to the next round.

The short track is about one-fourth the size of the long track.

The short track has tight turns. Skaters often touch the ice with a gloved hand. This helps them stay balanced around corners. They must also use **strategy** to stay in the race. When should they push ahead? When should they hold back? A mistake might send them crashing into another skater. If they fall, their chance of winning is over.

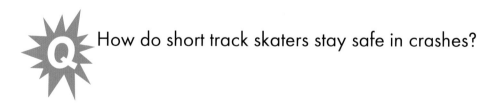 How do short track skaters stay safe in crashes?

High speed and a short track mean crashes happen in many races.

They wear helmets. They also wear pads on their elbows and knees. The track's walls are padded, too.

A skater from South Korea touches the ice to keep balance around a turn.

Short track skating includes three men's and three women's events for individual skaters. The shortest race is the 500 meter. Skaters go a little over four laps around the track. The longest race is the 1,500 meter. It takes 13.5 laps for a skater to reach the finish line.

 South Korea has won the most short track skating Olympic medals. But China and Canada are also top competitors.

Short track skating has one team race. It's a fast-paced sprinting **relay**. Each team has four skaters. One skater from each team is on the track. The teammates skate along inside the track. It's time for a hand off! The next skater moves onto the track just in front of her teammate. Shove! She starts her leg of the race. The fastest relay team wins gold.

Skaters shove their partners forward at the relay handoff.

Apolo Ohno celebrates winning the 500 meter race in the 2006 Olympics.

Go, Speed Racers!

Roar! A crowd loudly cheers for a blur of skaters. Speed skating is a popular sport. It's even getting a new long track event in 2018. The event is called the **mass start**. It will be raced like a short track event. Up to 24 skaters will race against one another for 16 exciting laps. It's just one more reason to stay tuned to the thrilling world of speed skating.

Glossary

air resistance The slowing force on a moving object as it moves through air.

long track The ice track used for the long track speed skating events; it is usually 400 meters (1,312 ft) for one lap.

mass start A long track speed skating event in which a big group of racers start at the same time, rather than holding heats of two racers at a time.

relay A race that a team of people do; each skater takes a turn completing part of the race.

short track The ice track used for short track speed skating events; it is usually 111.1 meters (364.5 ft) for one lap.

sprint To skate as fast as possible over a short distance.

strategy Careful planning and thoughtful choices used to reach a goal.

Read More

Barnas, Jo-Ann. *Great Moments in Olympic Skating.* Minneapolis: Sportszone, 2015.

Hunter, Nick. *The Winter Olympics.* Chicago: Heinemann-Library, 2014.

Hunter, Nick. *The World of the Olympics.* Chicago: Heinemann-Library, 2012.

Websites

Olympic Short Track Speed Skating
www.pyeongchang2018.com/horizon/eng/sports/Short_Track.asp?pgdiv=I#Short_Track

Olympic Speed Skating (long track)
www.pyeongchang2018.com/horizon/eng/sports/Speed_Skating.asp

US Speedskating
www.teamusa.org/us-speedskating

Index

air resistance 9

body position 9

equipment 9, 12, 13,
    22, 23

history 6, 7, 16, 17,
    24, 25

long track events 6,
    9, 10, 11, 12, 13,
    14, 17, 18, 19, 29

mass start event 29

men's events 6, 7, 14,
    17, 25

relays 26

safety 22, 23

short track events 6, 9,
    21, 22, 23, 24, 25,
    26, 29

team events 18, 19, 26

top countries 17, 25

women's events 6, 7,
    14, 17, 25

About the Author

Laura Hamilton Waxman has written and edited
many nonfiction books for children. She loves
learning about new things—like speed skating—
and sharing what she's learned with her readers.
She lives in St. Paul, Minnesota.

MAR 1 0 2018